How NOT TO Become A Little Old LADY

D0029103

How NOT to Become a Little Old LADY

Mary McHugh

Andrews McMeel Publishing®

Kansas City • Sydney • London

Andrews McMeel Publishing, LLC
an Andrews McMeel Universal company
1130 Walnut Street, Kansas City, Missouri 64106
www.andrewsmcmeel.com

15 16 17 18 19 WKT 22 21 20 19 18

ISBN: 978-0-7407-2213-4

Library of Congress Control Number: 2001053541

Illustrations copyright © 2002 by Adrienne Hartman
Book design by Holly Ogden

Attention: Schools and Businesses

Andrews McMeel books are available at quantity discounts with bulk purchase for educational, business, or sales promotional use. For information, please e-mail the Andrews McMeel Publishing Special Sales Department: specialsales@amuniversal.com.

INTRODUCTION

*I*t's one thing to grow older; it's quite another to wake up one morning and discover that you've turned into your Aunt Florence. What's wrong with Aunt Florence? Well, she hasn't exactly kept up with the times and, what's worse, she won't even try. She turns her back on computers and call waiting, and she clings to the familiar habits of the past that automatically identify her as a Little Old Lady.

The trouble with letting yourself become a Little Old Lady is that you are missing half the fun of being alive in the twenty-first century. Close your mind to any movie made after 1950, stop listening to music not played by a big band, cling to old friends and refuse to make new ones, and your life will be boring and stale.

I've always found the world a fascinating place, no matter how it changes, and, believe me, it has changed dramatically since I was born. There was no TV when I was a child, and now my grandsons have a satellite dish in Seattle so they can watch the Yankees. I never want to stop learning from people younger than I am. I want to keep on tap dancing in Macy's annual Tap-a-Thon with six thousand people every August. There is so much going on out there, and I don't want to miss any of it!

Creeping Little Old Lady-hood is everywhere, and every woman is vulnerable. How do you keep it from happening to you? Keep an eye out for these telltale signs.

Little Old Ladies...

Have never seen a ladies' room
that was clean enough.

Save grocery coupons,
which expire by the time they try
to use them.

Buy their clothes at garage sales
and don't notice the
food stains on them.

Think people will be surprised
when they tell them,
"I'm eighty-two years old."

Can produce pictures of
their grandchildren before
you get a chance to say hello.

Cackle instead of laugh.

Have tightly curled, scrunched-up
hairstyles left over from the '40s.

Talk about their bowel habits.

Consider ice cream a basic food group.

Pay no attention to the actual shape
of their lips when they put on lipstick.

Talk baby-talk to their cats
in front of strangers.

Still have a photographic memory—
they've just run out of film.

Say they don't need glasses and then
order the same thing in restaurants
every time because they
can't read the menu.

Say, "Everyone tells me I look
much younger than I am."

Talk about their root canals
during lunch.

Cover every surface of the
living room with little china
and glass figures that fall over
when you walk by them.

Try to exercise.

One Little Old Lady started walking five miles a day and no one has any idea where she is now.

Don't believe in cholesterol
and cook with tons of butter, cream,
and eggs.

Boil vegetables until they're gray.

Start every conversation with a stranger
by asking, "Where are you from?"
Then they say, "Oh, do you know
the Feldmans?"

Still expect people to RSVP
when they invite them to a party.

Tell long, boring stories with
no point to them.

Believe that there hasn't been
any music worth listening to
since Frank Sinatra died.

Would like men to wear jackets
and ties to restaurants and the theater,
and women to wear jewels
and high heels.

Still wear makeup and stockings
to the supermarket.

Dye their own hair and think
nobody can tell.

Who live in Florida can't stand
"all those old people who are
bad drivers."

Don't understand why their
grown children don't return their calls
the same day.

Remember when McDonald's hamburgers cost fifteen cents.

Watch soap operas and talk about the latest doings of Brad and Tiffany as if they were real people.

Smile when nothing is funny.

Have bristly chins.

Think everybody loves
Regis Philbin.

Can rest their breasts on their knees
without bending over.

Are proud they can't program
a VCR or use a computer.

Think microwaves fry your brain
if you stand near them.

Wish princess phones
would come back.

Refer to their stomachs as "tummies."

Don't know that girdles
are now called "Shapewear."

Fart in public.

Wish they would bring back hats
and gloves for everyday wear.

Who are Catholic still feel guilty
about eating meat on Friday.

Think there haven't been any real
movie stars since Joan Crawford died.

Wish Ma Bell would come back
and make the phones work again.

Think you're kidding when you
tell them there's a rock band called
"Post-Surgical Adhesions."

Still cook with lard.

Wonder why a two-pound box of candy
can make them gain five pounds.

Are shocked at the idea of
co-ed dorms.

Think nine dollars is an
outrageous price to pay for one
feature movie and four previews.

Won't wear white shoes before
Memorial Day or after Labor Day.

Try to pass off their liver spots
as large freckles.

Get drunk on one drink and tell you about
the man they *should* have married.

Can't call people by their first names
unless they've know them
for ten years.

Never let go of their handbags.

Are always crunching on
little hard candies.

Tell grandchildren stories
until everyone's eyes glaze over.

Refuse to give up their seat at the
slot machines in Atlantic City.

Think everyone at their
high school reunion looks older
and fatter than they do.

Think certain mirrors
make them look fat.

Haven't heard that nobody wears
bright blue eye shadow anymore.

Complain about the rain, young people,
music, lunch—everything!

Wear sleeveless dresses long after
their arms have started to flap.

Think all Spanish-speaking Americans
should stop it immediately and
learn English.

Get confused.

..☆...

When a travel agent told a Little Old Lady
that she would need a visa to travel to China,
she said, "Oh, no. I've been to China before
and they always accepted my
American Express card."

Never met a fattening dessert
they didn't like.

Think the rest of the world
should do what they do.

Wear plastic bonnets in the rain.

Make creaking noises
when they stand up.

Make their dogs wear sweaters when the
Little Old Lady feels cold.

Talk with their mouths full.

Flick on their signal twenty blocks
before they make the turn.

Have senior moments.

⋅⋅✬⋅⋅⋅

Two Little Old Ladies have been playing cards together for fifty years. One day, one of them says to the other, "Now don't get mad, but I've forgotten your name. What is it?" The other Little Old Lady glares at her for a couple of minutes and then says, "How soon do you need it?"

Repeat the same story
one hundred times.

Think Milton Berle in drag
was hilarious.

Refuse to get hearing aids
because they think everyone mumbles
and should speak up.

Turn on the left signal when
they're driving and then turn right.

Think they're fat because
of "glands."

Don't buy new clothes
until the old ones have fallen apart.

Who live in New York think
Hillary Clinton is pushy.

Talk about the preparations for
a colonoscopy during dinner.

Carry a complete assortment of snacks and cleaning products in their purses.

Think you are fascinated by what
they had for lunch yesterday.

Think it's cute to talk about
their "boyfriends."

Make annoying noises unwrapping
candy at the theater.

Hold up the whole line at the
supermarket counting out
exact change.

Call you "dearie" and "sweetie."

Refer to the refrigerator
as the "ice box."

Look like they're wearing seersucker
when they are naked.

Love the color blue because
it matches their hair and their veins.

Think everyone talks more softly now.

Think they're always right and
you're always wrong.

Make Christmas presents out of
empty milk cartons and
toilet paper rolls.

Miss Kathie Lee.

Think that there are times when
chocolate can solve all their problems.

Think URLs have something to do
with vacuum cleaners.

Wouldn't spend a Sunday
without Lawrence Welk on TV.

Make reservations for the
Early Bird Special.

Haven't gone to a movie since
The Sound of Music.

Think their hands will smell like gas
if they pump their own.

Never chew gum in public.

Swim with their entire heads out of
the water so their hair won't get wet.

Always say,
"I didn't sleep a wink last night."

Wear "dressmaker" bathing suits
with little skirts from 1954.

Ask their fifty-year-old children
if they have to go to the bathroom
before they leave the house.

Won't drink decaffeinated coffee
because they think it's still made
with Sanka.

Think wine and mixed drinks
make them drunk so they
drink straight gin.

Don't understand why anyone
would *pay* for water.

Wish long-distance operators
could actually find a number.

Think all Italians eat spaghetti
and are in the Mafia.

Are grateful their stomach covers
their flabby thighs.

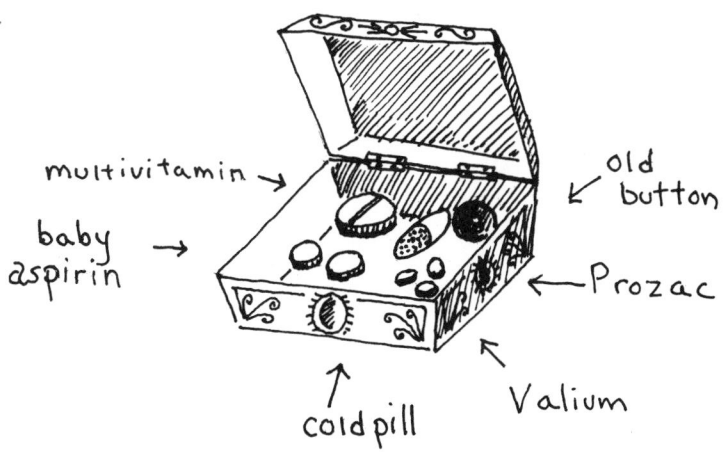

Never go anywhere without their pillbox.

Don't believe Rock Hudson was gay because he was so macho in *Pillow Talk* with Doris Day.

Hate voice mail, call waiting, answering machines, and computers.

Still call women over forty "girls."

Store their extra pots and pans
in the dishwasher.

Take half an hour to divide up
the bill in restaurants when they
have lunch with their friends.

Knit covers for their tissue boxes
and extra rolls of toilet paper.

Iron gift-wrapping paper and ribbons
and use them again.

Wonder whatever happened
to housedresses.

Stick rubber daisies on the bottom
of their bathtubs.

Still think their husbands
are always right.

Don't trust electronic deposits
and think ATM machines are an
invention of the devil.

Don't think any body part should be
pierced except the ears.

Have their hair done once a week
and don't shampoo it in between.

Consider a trip to the doctor
a social event.

Find it hard to talk into a
clown's mouth to get a hamburger.

Never like a menu the way it is printed.

Reuse bread bags.

Think "old" is ten years older
than whatever age they are.

Forget things.

·· ☆ ···

Three Little Old Ladies were discussing the problems of getting older. One said, "Sometimes I can't remember whether I meant to put the mayonnaise away or make a sandwich with it." The second said, "Sometimes I forget whether I started to go up the stairs or down." The third said, "Thank goodness I don't have those problems—knock on wood." She rapped on the table and said, "There's someone at the door. I'll get it."

Wear socks with high heels.

Remember when everyone sat around
and stared at the radio when
Edgar Bergen and Charlie McCarthy
were on.

Remember telephone party lines.

Reminisce about the days when you could mail a letter for three cents.

Remember when there was no
George Washington Bridge,
no Empire State Building, and
no Mickey Mouse.

Remember when you had to add
and subtract without a calculator.

Remember song lyrics that
rhymed "moon" and "June."

Remember when women cooked
every day.

Remember when you didn't kiss
on the first date.

Wear fur coats in April.

Snore and say it's their husband.

Make you look at all the pictures
they took on their trip
to Akron, Ohio.

Say, "I don't want to complain, but . . ."
and then they do.

Talk in loud whispers in theaters
and then glare when
you shush them.

Describe their vacations by what they ate.

Wear their reading glasses on a chain around their necks.

Wear their underpants until the elastic breaks and they fall off.

Still iron their husbands' undershorts.

Keep cooking deep-fried foods
even though their husbands are
one hundred pounds overweight.

Think that a Croque Monsieur
is a death sentence in France.

Consider their husbands'
swearing at other drivers
a sign of masculinity.

Think nobody should say "vagina"
out loud and they certainly shouldn't
write a play about it.

Drive twenty-three mph
in a twenty-five mph zone.

Still stick their hand out the window
to signal.

Loudly whisper things like
"They're very wealthy, you know" or
"He has prostate cancer."

Tell complete strangers embarrassing
things about their grown children,
as in, "Betsy wet her pants the
first day of kindergarten."

Get common sayings just a
little bit wrong: "I wouldn't trust him
with a ten-foot pole" or "He's made
money hand over heels."

Take it personally when Hawaiians
say "Hang loose."

Refer to pregnancy as a woman being
"in trouble" or "in a family way."

Love to drive slowly in
the fast lane.

Tell you about every single flower
they planted in their garden.

Think the wrinkles in their ankles
are in their stockings.

Still ask "Where is the ladies' room?"
in a place with unisex bathrooms.

Think cell phones should be banned.

Have too much room in the house and
not enough room in the medicine cabinet.

Don't comb their hair in public—
they pat it.

Bend over to pick something up and
then try to think of something else to do
while they're down there.

Carry a tissue in every pocket
or up their sleeves.

Wear knee-high stockings with
above-the-knee dresses.

Say "That's nice, dear," when you
tell them your dog died, because they
didn't really hear you.

Need glasses to find their glasses.

Think people who live in California
are all hippies or gay.

Still think you can take appliances
somewhere to be fixed.

Can't always keep up.

· · ⭐ · · ·.

A husband said to his wife,
"Honey, let's go upstairs and make love,"
and she said, "I don't know if I can do both."

Think therapy is a hoax—
you just have to take a good look
at yourself.

Talk about people no one else
has ever heard of.

Need things explained.

A Little Old Lady called her travel agent and asked, "Do airlines put your physical description on your bag so they know whose luggage it is?" The agent said, "No, why do you ask?" The little old lady replied, "Well, when I checked in at the airport at Fresno, they put a tag on my luggage that said FAT, and I'm overweight." The travel agent explained that the city code for Fresno is FAT, and that the airline didn't really think she was obese.

Use so much hair spray a tornado
couldn't mess their "do."

Wish we could go back to
everything being "pleasant."

Think women are failures
if they aren't married with children.

Think gas should still cost
thirty cents a gallon.

Think the president should make
more money than ballplayers.

Think all mothers should stay home
with their children.

Don't tell their age.
They say, "I've just celebrated
the third anniversary of my
twenty-fifth birthday."

Say, "I'll just have one piece," and then
eat half the box of candy.

Still try to change their husbands.

A Little Old Lady went to the doctor to ask his help in reviving her husband's sex drive. He suggested Viagra, but she said he wouldn't even take an aspirin for a headache. "Drop it in his coffee," the doctor said. A week later she came back and the doctor asked how things went. "It was terrible!" she said. "What happened?" the doctor asked. "Well, I dropped it in his coffee like you said, and he jumped up, ripped off his clothes, and made love to me right on the table. It was terrible!" "Why?" the doctor asked. "I'll never be able to show my face in McDonald's again!" she said.

Turn to the obituary page first and
are relieved when they don't
see their name.

Wonder who that wrinkly old lady
in the mirror is.

Buy purses with zippered pockets
and forget what's in each pocket.

Accuse their husbands of taking
their keys when they lose them.

Keep looking for
The Ed Sullivan Show on TV.

Think long-distance phone calls
should be saved for something
earth-shaking, like the birth of a baby
or the death of a relative.

Can never remember their
license numbers even when they have
vanity plates.

Forget which side of the mall
they parked their car on and
think someone stole it.

Are convinced that manufacturers put the wrong sizes on clothing these days because size 6 doesn't fit them anymore.

Can't understand how somebody
can go to a large city by herself
and not be raped and murdered.

Wear "safe" colors like beige,
ecru, and taupe.

Still think "gay" means cheerful.

Always sit in the aisle seat on airplanes because they have to go to the bathroom five times during a two-hour flight.

Still say "telegraph poles"
instead of "telephone poles."

Call the front porch the "stoop."

Have more doctors' phone numbers
than friends' in their address books.

Head for the bathroom
at the sound of running water.

Wear jeweled harlequin sunglasses
from the '40s.

Love the newspaper feature
called "25 Years Ago Today."

Think ZIP codes are just another way
to make life more difficult.

Wish telephone exchanges still had
lovely names like Butterfield 8
and Plaza 9.

Think they have insomnia
when they can't get back to sleep
at four A.M. after going to bed at 8:30.

Use up every last smidgin of toothpaste
before they throw out the tube.

Have canned goods older
than their grandchildren.

Wet their pants when they sneeze.

Keep waiting for someone who dials a wrong number to say, "I'm sorry."

Should open their windows once in a while to let those twenty-year-old smells out.

Don't understand how they can
hang something in their closet for
six months and it shrinks two sizes.

Want to punch skinny people who say
"Sometimes I just forget to eat."

Think the symptoms of stress—
eating too much and impulse buying—
are their idea of a perfect day.

Know what Victoria's Secret is—
nobody who weighs more than
ninety-seven pounds or is older than
thirty can fit into their stuff.

Let their husbands do the driving
and worry the whole time that he
will kill both of them.

Buy everything on the
Home Shopping Network.

Are somewhere between the
Age of Consent and the Age of Collapse.

Still remember candy cigarettes.

Think the print in newspapers and books is getting smaller and smaller every year.

Wish we could go back to a time
when the worst thing you could catch
from the opposite sex was cooties.

Remember when having a weapon
in school was being caught
with a slingshot.

Call their grown children to tell them
they woke up in the middle of
the night with chest pains and will ask
the doctor about it when they
see him next month.

Wonder why policemen, doctors,
and ministers are so young.

Think "on-line" means not using your
clothes dryer and a that a floppy
is a sagging body part.

Think you can catch cold
by getting your feet wet.

Will tell you that everything hurts
and what doesn't hurt, doesn't work.

Wish that just once someone
would ask for proof when they request
a senior citizen ticket at the movies
or on a train.

Save rubber bands.

Have elastic waistbands on all their slacks.

Are absent-minded.

One Little Old Lady asked her husband to go to the kitchen and bring her some ice cream with whipped cream and chocolate sauce. He came back with a plate of scrambled eggs and bacon and she said, "You forgot the toast."

Often start a sentence with
"Now in *my* day . . ."

How Not to Become a Little Old Lady

Do you (or someone you love) have any of these symptoms?